Shore Ordered Ocean

Shore Ordered Ocean

Dora Malech

[signature]

For Bryan!

[signature] Dora

WAYWISER

2016

First published in 2009 by

THE WAYWISER PRESS

Bench House, 82 London Road, Chipping Norton, OX7 5FN, UK
P.O. Box 6205, Baltimore, MD 21206, USA
http://waywiser-press.com

Editor-in-Chief
Philip Hoy

Senior American Editor
Joseph Harrison

Associate Editors
Dora Malech Eric McHenry V. Penelope Pelizzon Clive Watkins Greg Williamson

Reprinted 2014

A CIP catalogue record for this book is available from the British Library

ISBN 978-1-904130-39-0

Printed and bound by
Printondemand-worldwide.com,
9 Culley Court, Orton, Southgate, Peterborough PE2 6XD

for Harry and Emily

Acknowledgements

Thanks to the editors of the following journals and anthologies that first published these poems:

Best New Poets 2007: "A Shortcut"
The Canary: "Push, Pull"
Forklift, Ohio: "Fittest, Survival of"
Gulf Coast: "Highways Are Abandoned"
Kaupapa: New Zealand Poets/Global Issues: "Caretaking", "Still Life with Bodies and Land", "Witness"
LIT: "One Time She Held My Head While I Threw Up Gin on Her Tiles"
The New Yorker: "Here Name Your", "Let the Record Show"
Poetry: "Makeup", "Treasure Hunting"
Poetry London: "City Beach", "Fair Play", "Heaven"
Poet Lore: "An Old Story"
The Sonora Review: "With a Scattered Chance of Forecast"
Sport: "A Way", "Drought Year", "Here and There", "Let Me Explain", "Liar", "Places, Places"
Tight: "The Eel"
Turbine: "And Made of It", "Dreaming in New Zealand", "Floral Arrangements", "Long Distance", "Missive", "Ponte Sisto", "Safe Passage", "The Up-and-Up", "You Are Here"

Thanks to the editors of *Best New Zealand Poems 2007* for including the poem "Dreaming in New Zealand".

The author gratefully acknowledges the assistance of Yale College and the Frederick M. Clapp Trust, the University of Iowa Writers' Workshop and the Truman Capote Literary Trust, Glenn Schaeffer and the Glenn Schaeffer Award in Poetry, the Civitella Ranieri Foundation and Center, the Breadloaf Writers' Conference, and Victoria University's International Institute of Modern Letters.

The author also thanks the following individuals: Elizabeth Alexander, Connie Brothers, Sarah German, Joseph Harrison, Brenda Hillman, Philip Hoy, James Galvin, Mark Levine, Dan Malech, Dana Prescott, Jacob Root, John Root, Cole Swensen, Jan Weiss-miller, and Dean Young.

Contents

Contents

Let Me Explain

Spring, and the tulips urged me
stick to schedule, flower furiously.
I asked for mountains but settled
for some flood-buckled linoleum.
Air was the only sure thing
and even she put up a fight.
I called my eyes near-sighted,
my hands near misses, my arms
close calls, my face old hat,
my head a bluff and raised
my body, a wishing machine.
Stars, thanked. Days, numbered.
I wore a coat because you can't trust
weather and I looked like rain.

A Shortcut

A hedgehog shuffles out to take a moment
of the moon. The moon leaves off trying on
cloud after cloud to render for a moment
the frowsy foliage and the nose beneath
in tenebrous strokes, not light and dark,
but light in dark or light in spite of.
Doesn't rinse the brush to touch the lilies'
brief white swash and sticky spots
of seeds and pulp where the karakas bend
and drop their drupes. Sprays of stone-fruit
come to sweet rot underfoot with a stench
that in a warmer, brighter hour would draw
the flies to feed at each smear adhered, here
to the asphalt switchback and there to the stairs
that teeter through the terraces and past
the walls that prop the city up above the sea,
walls studded with snails after a day of rain.
The young snails resemble pearl barley, pale,
scattered as at some strange matrimony,
the old are dark burls grown somehow from brick.
Egalitarian spectrum renders the memory
of the sun's gaudy palette obsolete
here where each edge is a glint and each
hollow, a shadow. Holds at first glance each
as distant and as dear, though an eye that waits
to warm to, lets its iris open into
finds that though both take a glimmer, the shell
knows one way to shine and the body, another.
The former's luster, a crystal ball in which
one sees the muddy future, the latter,
a small brown tongue pronouncing "like" against
a concrete palate, careful. Only the wind hurries
here, and the leaves turn aside to let it pass,
shake disapproval. A spider rests

after mending its nets, sits at the center
of tenuous nebula wound from catkin
to fern frond to the black beaks of the last flax,
an almost-still-life. Here a twitch and there
a shiver and each snail's nacreous wake
belies if not progress then process,
illuminated glyphs, transient text, a glisten
spelling if not here-to-there then
somewhere-to-somewhere
by way of these walls that hold the hills from
their someday certain spill into the harbor
a moment more and then another moment
more for each of our small sakes.

Here Name Your

My friend spends all summer
mending fence for the elk to blunder

back down and the cows to drag
the wires and the snow to sit and sag

on, so all the twist and hammer and tauten
and prop amounts at last to nought, knot, tangle.

The next year he picks
up his pliers and fixes

the odds all over again. There are no
grownups, and I think that all of us children know

and play some variation on this theme, the game of all join
hands so that someone can run them open.

Then war whoops, shrieks, and laughter
and re-gather together

as if any arms might ever really hold.
I'm trying to finger the source – pleasure of or need

for – these enactments of resistance, if Resistance
is indeed their name. I'm trying to walk the parallels to terminus –

call them lickety-split over rickety bridge,
tightrope, railroad tie, or plank as you see fit –

trying to admit to seeing double,
innumerable,

to finding myself beset by myself
on all sides, my heart forced by itself,

for itself, to learn not only mine
but all the lines –

crow's flight, crow's-feet, enemy, party, picket,
throwaway, high tide, and horizon – to wait

in the shadows of scrim each night
and whisper the scene. Always, some part

of the heart must root for the pliers, some
part for the snow's steep slope.

And Made of It

East, enter potter under
whose hands the world
turns clockwise.

West, counterclockwise,
say *tradition* meaning
means nothing,

no blown breath nor big pull.
In the name of *is what it is,*
sun casts the shadows

as themselves for a change.
To speak to into or to
through this needs more

than my little muscles.
Perhaps a handle.
An *as if* turned to music,

slurry sieved to slip.
Here are my hands
for pulling the walls up.

Here is the air
will cause a wobble.
Rib to tip in the direction

of rotation, murmur,
momentum, *tell you
What. I tell you What.*

Centered, I am ready
for an opening.
But for a throw of,

or thrown off, or
to or for or from.
Kick throw repeat

is my prayer
for a pliable vessel.
I have never seen

a child unquiet
while watching
the wheel.

Aleph, Bet

In my favorite version, the man recites the alphabet
over and over, and when asked, he says he is praying.
He admits he lacks the words, but says perhaps if he provides
enough letters, God can piece his purpose back together.

The word is *kavanah*, translates to *concentration* or *intent*,
without which, the words lie inert. And with? Call it *all rise*.
The urge made agent, leavens the lips, tongue, throat, and eyes.
In other words, heart's *yes*, yeast, or likens to, likewise lives,

needs no light to grow. What say the brewer and baker?
What of the grapes in the sun with the *yes* on their skin,
the *blush* or *bloom*? And what of this *yes*'s twin, the, as they say,
opportunistic pathogen? I don't believe I know. I'd like to ask

someone who knows, summon my strongest letters together and say:
How long do you think you knew before you knew you knew? Or
    rather,
how long do you think you think you knew before you dressed
your *I guess* in the *yes* you said *I do* to, to know you know now?

Treasure Hunting

Soon to be a low moon and elsewhere
fire. Lucky mountain shone copper
but not to pocket. Not that kind of angel

between maybe and the blaze. Asked
to hold my baby. Didn't envy gravity
to lug its chubby moon from under.

Dear dire said the radio and oh I was
its girl. Called it a silver un-bridge
a single listing trestle. Someday sounded

the siren of a false all-clear. May I?
My skein all un-spun under fire.
The spider alive in a primrose.

The baby bent to an iris and willing
her face to unfurl. I wanted to watch
the coupling trains. Had never seen

machines in love before. No arrowheads
but among ordinary stones red flint from
which one had maybe once been broken.

The sky streaks with diurnal war paint.
Touches on baby's pulse where
a dream tries to surface. Touches

as the horsemen do (indeed) pass by
the monarch in said spider's web
where struggles spin to filigree.

Makeup

My mother does not trust
women without it.
What are they not hiding?
Renders the dead living

and the living more alive.
Everything I say sets
the clouds off blubbering
like they knew the pretty dead.

True, no mascara, no evidence.
Blue sky, blank face. Blank face,
a faithful liar, false bottom.
Sorrow, a rabbit harbored in the head.

The skin, a silly one-act, concurs.
At the carnival, each child's cheek becomes
a rainbow. God, grant me a brighter myself.
Each breath, a game called Live Forever.

I am small. Don't ask me to reconcile
one shadow with another. I admit –
paint the dead pink, it does not make
them sunrise. Paint the living blue,

it does not make them sky, or sea,
a berry, clapboard house, or dead.
God, leave us our costumes,
don't blow in our noses,

strip us to the underside of skin.
Even the earth claims color
once a year, dressed in red leaves
as the trees play Grieving.

S.O.S.

Despite the ray of forecast, another battery of storms.
Half-a-minute's blue respite complete with lowered length of
    rainbow
soon snatched back to becloud and awash.

Wind-struck, each drop lists and cringes, picks itself up
to feint mid-air, then fall again. No such luck of alee anywhere,
trees keen to tear their garb funereal, in every crack, the wail and
    whistle,
and sirens across the bay where some soul braved it, bit the slick.
Sure, sob's a sodden sell, but try – I try – me.

Dilute the delusion's all I'll concede to "coming to my senses,"
in love as I am with one beyond further than far off past the
    thither side
of a real void's void, though, so, today, it seems, is every other
    castaway here sloshing
selfsame the shipwrecked streets apace, each face puddle-ward
    and each head's crown
an advance thrust first formation, not to bruise a gust or best, but
    simply to weather
aweather, as each makes do in just the one allotted body.

Delivery Rhyme

for Alyssa

As anyone
is apt to, you began as someone

else's symptom. As in
other beginnings: drawn lots, blood,
some dancing on the heads of pins

and inside needles' eyes,
cellular revelry,

hopping
of microscopic

turnstiles. Lucky guest,
grist, leapt

long odds to spark
the tinder in the dark.

Then, the subcommittees met:
made merry in duplicate, triplicate

and so on, much of themselves, divided
and divined and concurred.
All sides insides, pre-ambulatory
perambulation meant: sure

ambit, short orbit
in a warm aquarium set

to the muffled music of a single sphere.
As in other beginnings: parting seas, the future's
violent egress, screams and sutures,

aftermath's average agony
on umbilical belay

but soon to solo, unfold all
those origami limbs to test
the inevitable debutante bawl.

Wrest from the nest
and the rest is you, dear:
dressed for the bright lights
in bits of my sister.

Going Somewhere

Last night I stepped off the porch to see the moon
and saw that satellite connect the dots again,
her blink and lurch lit on, lit off and on.
What was ever meant by *out* or *all the stops*
or *pulling* for that matter, by no news is goodbye

by good lie by godspeed notwithstanding?
Today's wind was a stutter, bore stops and starts,
tumbles of op eds and eleventh innings, fliers,
feathers, string turned tangled from gutter to gutter
and over the dead cat flattened from fur to a banner

of brown blood by cars crossing the river bridge.
Today's sky was as many as seven eagles,
loitering in the bare branches, gone by noon.
Inside, Question & Answer lasted until two
while the sun puddled in the folding chairs

and the old hinges announced late arrivals
and early departures. I stood in the back
and rocked heel toe heel toe, tried to believe
in the shortest distance between posit and possess,
wanted the wise one to utter *eke* and also

long time coming. Motes mid-voyage and sneezes
and a truck bleating about backward motion
in the alley outside. Why did the provost shift
as she did at *ever after*? I raised my hand
but wasn't asked to ask.

Good Neighbors

Each pane, a glass axe
in waiting. Each true axe
leaned on the casing, asleep

by the door upside down.
Wind in our belongings.
Scatters empties in the grass.

Claims it lost something
the last time. Dust, smoke,
sure, but not this hat.

From here to, you know,
a big bit for grit teeth.
Slow motion's still

motion so I insist
we're *getting there.*
I would call us good

neighbors, but don't ask
the flies. They're waiting
for blood on everything.

One Time She Held My Head
While I Threw Up Gin on Her Tiles

All the sissies commit
the names of flowers to memory
crying *larkspur, aster, beebalm* in the dark.
Let me remind you that he shot her in the face.
At the Funland Redemption Center,
the woman reassures me I can trade
my rings and teddies for something
much, much larger. I tell myself,
inside a head is another, smaller head –
think of the mascot, his desperate
half-time dance. I long for the dank privacy
of the bear suit, want to rest my cheeks
between my two enormous paws.
The old love songs peel away
their masks to reveal dirges,
moaning *everybody loves to cha cha cha*.
The ancients believed bump and grind
would ward off death. This is not about
death, rather, that he shot her in the face.
Her body wants its head back.
I dare you to bend low, explain
the mechanics of expiring meat.
The sky and soil hold her down:
Ma'am, we're just doing our job.
Nobody laugh, but you can feel
whatever else you want.

Our Bearings

Still-dark hills and silver harbor
for a vanity, the sky indulges
in mauve, in peach, in cornflower,
tracery, tulle, flimsy effulgence
never to weather a day.

The only constant coordinates here
are the going and the gone, axis
atilt without lodestone or polestar,
leeward a fancy, windward a whim.

Navigate as such, but take first cue
from this eternal ingénue who cossets
what ephemera will fit to tatters
again and to tatters again in tea rose,
in tangerine, in violet, inviolate.

Ubi Sunt

Where is the lookout
over where
the rivers meet?
Where is the weave
of canopy and sky?
Here there is fog
and a thin path.
Tread threads tract
to contract, acts
as line and signer.
Where is a promise
that's firmer than
strangers' desire?
Hisses trust,
die that's stamped
a snake-scape.
Earth burnished
by a shared need.

I hear the bird
that ululates,
but where?
Soil, steeped
in a week's rain,
slips to show
the map
the roots
have wrought,
legend-less tangle
of byways, inroads,
turnabout,
somewhere over
or without form,
which is not

to say
nowhere,
which is to say
not here.

Heaven

It is a fire we are almost sure we
have caught in time. Although we did not see
the strike, we now imagine that we heard
its thunder louder than the rest as we
slept back to back and woke to swim into
each other. Drove a sweet-smelling scar down
the trunk to smolder in the needles, call in
backup from the wind. It is not the house
on fire, nor is it no fire at all. We have
shovels and are running toward it together.

Scenic Overlook

The field's perimeter – expiring lilacs.
Two brothers fight over the spool

of a kite that remains aloft.
In my tent I sleep on my sweater

and dream only of myself. I want
to be an *enthusiast* when I grow up.

Knickers kick on a windy line.
Blossoms fall on a trampoline.

The wind takes its share of magnolias,
still calyx-bound, now – enter feet – underfoot.

Someone has hung a plastic raptor to bank
and bob a dizzy warning over the seedlings

and dark-turned dirt. The sun plays
a game called Spin to Gold.

In one language, *time* is a synonym for *season*.
In one language, *vengeance*, for *answer*.

A favorite fallacy: objects at rest.
I swear I never meant to dream this way.

Did I mention the lilacs? The brothers?
Okay, let's talk about something else.

You Are Here

Body's gallon and a half of blood – he knew
but hadn't told me yet. Hung right, lurched
over tracks. Said he loved Bartholomew –
flipped, flayed, lugging his skin. The birches
played yes-men, nodded off. Beyond the trees,
a woman tried to teach her dog to sic.
The sound of the jerked choke chain carried
rattle of metal links. Claim dark led our lips
to an undisclosed location. Branches heavy,
fallen on a wire. Some train had an answer
to *define absolve,* but too far off. See,
we didn't see the gun-shy stars until much later.
Three gallons, good moon. *Good dog, now sit.*
He touched his tongue to where my lip was split.

Liar

This is where we learn how to approach disparate conflagrations, a flaming television, say, versus a flaming pile of oil-soaked rags. They play the clip of the burning stadium as our punishment or our reward, "Your time will come" or else a "Thank you for your time," I can't be sure. "Now see the people who believe they can escape up top," they say, "Now count the seconds 'til that roof falls in." One. Two. A man runs out onto the field, his back and arms ablaze and chased by their own lit wake. Others push him down and wave their jackets over him. "They're only drawing in more oxygen to feed the flames," they say. They hit his body with their jackets. "The right idea," they say, "But by now the heat has melted what's inside his arms and the blows are breaking the burnt skin that's holding him together." An audible hiss of breath took in at our collective wince. "Don't worry," they say, "A man like that's in shock. He doesn't even know that he's on fire."

Places, Places

A mistranslation gave Moses
his horns and they stuck.
What you see is what we are –
ignominious physiognomy,
our lumps writ large. At the party,
the drunk surgeon moans *I've seen
the human heart*. No zoo's a bestiary.
Even the greatest sometimes paint
an awfully heavy halo. On behalf
of our hands, the pugilist puppets
go at it, Pulcinella giving the Devil
what for. Behind the scrim, a man,
and now his hands are kissing.
Ask if he's Pulcinella and he'll say
if only. The overeager guidebook
claims *the fish is tastiest when it looks
like nothing you've seen before,*
claims *masks were worn year round
in the time of the Republic.*
Imagine the words of the wives:
Dear, you're not wearing that *face,
are you?* I'd like to think I'd give
what for. I'd like to think that mine's
a heart-shaped face and written all over.
No reliquary's mine to regulate
and if one were I wouldn't.
Perhaps what's under glass is not
the finger that touched the wound
but it's certainly a finger.

Here and There

Perhaps not real head and real wall this time.

After the endless season of condolences,
come to to the sound of the neighbor muttering
what a boring dulcimer that was.

Our hero is burning the sheaves of shorthand,
asked and answered and oyez and so forth,
letting the estimable elders down.

The river's becoming a torrent of blossoms.

The hands wish to be read their rights again.

Perhaps it's time to think of savings, press
the pansies in the atlas, wet the thread
to take arms against the needle's tricky eye.

Bequeathed to our bodies, a decent descent.

Our hearts are teething. Our friends won't let us
drive them on the highways anymore.

More terror in a *meanwhile* or a *yet*?

We say *too much* until the words dissolve,
a city of girls wearing white in the rain.

Breaking News

As if the lucky might ride it to shore
while the others go under.

Some dogs make for higher ground,
spurred by a shake or a sound
in a frequency to which we never tuned.

Dogs' ears rise now
to the scream of the still-black screen,
the pitch before the picture.

Breaking here means broken elsewhere.
All our instruments, and still we're late.

It's six o'clock. In the windows,
families flicker on,
faces splashed blue in the wake.

Highways Are Abandoned

My friend bends the microphone's neck to his mouth,
stands among strangers in folding chairs and speaks

of his sadness. *Good job*, my friend and *good girl*
to the dog, circling and squatting so low to the lawn.

Today I drove past two men strung from trees with yellow rope,
suspended as they sawed down branches. When I passed

back I saw only rope, no men, four police cars, two ambulances.
I know a blackjack dealer who says *better lucky than good*

each time she flips my cards. In the newspaper, brimstone,
a girl whispering *at first I thought it was a joke, then they started*

to shoot the windows. I can't be the only one wondering
about the whereabouts of our gold medals, our arms to end

all open arms. *Good night* to my sister, whose bed I shared
when we were small. Each night *good night* and turned our backs.

When I am at a loss for words I try *ravage, havoc, clemency.*
Good luck to my mother, hauling her lump in to the doctors.

Once on a train a woman tried to give me twenty dollars
to make me stop crying.

Push, Pull

Coughed and called what bled the quick.
One kick, one trick, one act, one hit.

Called the troops less precious few.
To lift a fist and strike a deal.

To best the jester, cheek to lodestone.
Not rising was occasion of its own.

Spring brought a stiff rain of prostheses,
the storm's black eye on our procession

draped in lace, hook, line, and I do.
Meant charred limbs, rest in pieces.

Meant long time came and none too quiet.
Then, too quiet beneath the birthing

of new galaxies, the nebula's
dark arms of dust. Sun smoldered on.

Baby's first words were friendly fire.
Chrysanthemums of copper wire.

Cat buried out back in a satin hatbox
beside my big broken, obsolete token

I'd taken to wearing on a string. Tried
to trade, but the wind wouldn't bargain, took

more than her fair share of starlings,
left me kneeling on the tarmac,

mouth full of ammo and ipecac,
strange heart in my throat, a belly of swelling.

Bells on bridles to ready for battle.
Broke those horses and there weren't any

horses left. Explosives in the hope chest.
Hawks waiting to be whistled off the fist.

Doused the dovecotes with gasoline.
Slipped the last dowels from the cask.

Couldn't we call the crash a birdbath?
Couldn't we call the coffins gift wrap?

Must have been some misunderstanding.
Shore ordered ocean but sent it back.

With a Scattered Chance of Forecast

Unstrung, the fence posts list which way
and every like a drunken firing squad.
I'd like to say they'll never hit us, but.
Or see our swaying as an isolated breeze
and not what's coming. This week's gods
are bored even by blood and not above
tough love, a brick's hard kiss, accelerator.
Someone insists velocity is virtue. Someone
defines amen as keep-it-coming. There is no
wisest way to wait for strangers. I would not
mend of my own accord, miss my wire either.
Not breath as in bait, but our bracing, a bit.
Unstrung, the fence posts lean down toward
the dust as if listening into approach. Not yet,
but the tree, in turn, holds all its little breaths.
Humble ambassador to that high window.
Someone's children unafraid behind the glass.

The Up-and-Up

There is infinite precedent
for the perversion of clemency.
I have held the envelope up to the light.

When the President pardons a guilty man,
clouds the color of the night sky cover
most of the night sky, and the remaining

stars seem to huddle together.
This is one of many pet projections,
I admit, to fancy the fires

of far off encampments and each
with a single sleepy sentry
not unlike myself.

No weapons, no maidens,
no vessels, no beasts.
Actually, exactly like myself,

how mirrors catch and cast,
flash back, at last, a hopeful signal.
The less I can identify the constellations,

the more I identify with them.
Call it cathexis, a false positive,
or New Moon, another name

for looks like nothing now but wait.
I have tried to compose myself.
When the coroner handed me the watch,

I couldn't look, unsure if I'd rather find
it stopped at the time of or still telling.
I live by the fault line, infirm firmament's

faithful child. Outside, the two-faced grove
bows one way and the other, opens its cones
first for rain and then for flame,

annulling the trunk where I offered
my mark, where the live wood healed
to a black love knot, proof of conscription.

I saw hands break both haft and hasp
to axe the hatch and burn the last
bridge at both ends. Perhaps

I should have shook them, grateful.
Instead, I practiced casting shadows,
flat stones in the hope of the day they find

me blameless. I have prayed, and pray,
for a patient anthropologist
to teach me how to be myself again.

Let the Record Show

I spent the morning trying to remember
the joke about a peanut and assault.
People dropped bombs on each other elsewhere.
I knew that many of them were at fault

and many blameless. I kept my office locked
and the lights off. The phone just kept ringing.
I didn't answer. Nor when someone knocked.
I was supposed to be doing something.

Drought Year

Even the sky has its hobbies, cirrus, etcetera.
Cannot rain every day and these days any day

can not rain. The sage and I play
sought and found. I am an amateur

and try to keep my blue above the skyline.
Talk of monitoring elsewhere's mountain,

sighs out of ash, and the meteors' signatures.
Mama puts all her eggs in one chimney again.

A plan for a plan. So breaks our oldest news.
Silence, though "not the void and not contentment,"

where wind writes the grass into yellow italics
and the sky dabbles in sunsets, violent festoonery,

faiblesse. It is the minister of the interior.
I can draw lovely flowers and terrible hands.

Change

What was left
after the price
of gas
not much
in the ARCO
station outside
Desert Springs
discount fountain pop
a toilet tank
with a brick but no
handle cholla spines
whose barbs held
fast to the cracks
in the linoleum
a mirror in which
someone had scraped
Please Wash Hands
to Please   ash
gold dust
on the floor
rather regular
dust the sun
slanted golden
silver scratch-off
ticket dust sloughed
on the counter
a pen on a chain
and a Planter's can
with a slit stabbed
through its plastic
lid a nickel
for the slit above
the hand-written

request Please
Help Us Bury
Our Baby.

Still Life with Bodies and Land

See our rubble rising from the coast,
the burning grove, winnowing wind of chaff,
ash, scaffolding, and refuse to inure to.

Divining rod, refusing refuge, lists
to the sea.

                    See, we're both bleeding.
Hold my wound to yours and call us a family.

Some times call for simpler symbols.
If *this* is *this* then that's that, you see.

Never as simple as weapon of choice.
Why waste good blood? That splinter's still in there.
Skin knows no words for entreat, retreat, treaty.

What will burn we will burn. We are bound
by what we will not will, what of our own
we will destroy before surrender. Dear,
keep what you wish of me.
                              How to auger
birds on fire?

              See me still standing sentry
over the breakwater where the night weeps
like a licked stitch.

                    Cannot trust our slim psalms,
cannot trust our shunts or cantilevers.
Consider this an offering.
Insist on viscera, velocity.

Beneath
oath and fire, find my fingers, blue feathers,
fresh water, and, with luck, the rest of me.

Witness

For the jury's sake please state the make
and model of the ultimatum.
All eyes on the midnight shift,

gauntlet of ghost crabs. Lodged in my throat,
a formal complaint. Summer begot winter.
Winter begot winter. I suspected something

when I saw the rain of fire.
Missed muster, split crosshairs,
signed the writ but smudged the fine print

clear down the dotted line. Hint:
thou shalt not. Small song of scattered ash
and enter countermelody –

a tisket, a tasket, last picnic, last basket –
a tisket, a turbine, a tisket, a target,
a tisket, a towline, a tisket, a tomb.

Shelve the self for a second.
Yesterday, a pillory. Chastened continuum.
Today, gray tourniquet.

Tomorrow, lovely weather
to identify the body. Please pass
the pillar, the puppets, the public address.

Sforzando. A nexus of angels.
Slashed the palms to seek their fortunes.
All the censers at a standstill.

Wet dogs cowering before thunder.
God gives us heavy hands and takes
attendance: Benson? Eckenrode? Holter? Swindell?

Caretaking

She's not my baby, but she's sleeping.
Static on the monitor.

Thunder in winter, the sky turned
inward, speaking only of herself again.

Acetylene torches weld the manhole covers
shut along the route of the inaugural parade.

I'm mostly made of water.
What's your excuse?

Baby's job is to breathe.
My job is to watch baby breathe.

Ready, set, loiter at the cloister.
I am one of the lucky ones, allowed

to borrow a face to pray for for the day.
Answers to today's puzzle include *loss of life,*

laugh out loud, heir to the thrall
and on the opposing page, the Specialist

of the hour tells us *we're going to find out
what kind of monster I am today.*

Degrees of debris: thimbles, shrapnel,
the metal case holding twenty glass eyes.

In comes the airplane.
Pray for a thumb in every mouth

but don't bother bribing History with gifts.
She has everything she came for already.

Fittest, Survival of

Seduction by fire, for fire.
By distance, by poultice,

seduction by swaying
and what a show we were –

all the tumblers trussed
in the tightrope, tangle

of hooks and crooks and nannies,
sons of the nuns and the dry drunks,

sons called "Off the Search,"
sons called "It a Day,"

and "The End" always a crocodile.
This is not a cancer but further

evaluation is recommended
for the reassurance that something

of more concern is not present.
Marching orders: go disfigure.

Press zero to speak to an operator
or just say *help*. Fly on the wall

for lobotomists' shop talk,
old tongue's new trick tries

"kanflu-greyshun" on for size.
"Oo" as in boot, "ur" as in urge.

This heat-seeking scope
is a dream in the bedroom.

We've let baby call the wolf
a woof-woof for too long.

Sick kitty's pity party mewling
what remains? What remains –

questions for corpses.
Shameless angels flaunting their empties.

Percussion, repercussion,
ahem, amen, a pause,

applause, exit stage left.
God won't miss six swans and a heron.

Presupposition, presupplication.
There was a time when the river

could have forgiven, wanted nothing
more than for us to wade in and start singing.

Safe Passage

Here is the cat. Here is the cradle.
Here is the bird that cries *to-do*
and where your daughter
passed through the frozen season,
the empty house. *I love you*
in the film that collects on the table,
on the windowpanes. Where she ran
her fingers through your dust and frost.

Here, the man with his goose and his fox
reduced to a smudge with a speck and a dot,
having safely crossed the river.
In the fallen city, the surprise was
what was *not* found, which was
virtually anything. Porch guarded
by a gun called Kindness. Small dogs
at the screen doors, big dogs at the gates.

We'll hear what's coming if it's coming.
Not alone, see, rather, *beside myself.*
When all of my lines are lines of defense.
When all of our best suits outfit the dead.
Same scale of one to stricken. The clauses
include: Stop-gap. Sunset. Here, my straight
face claiming victory, trimming the wicks
to praise what is ours to re-ravel.

Not *felled* city. Fallen. Where men
no older than yourself stood in the sun,
but trembling. We used to say *my people*,
knew which wind would carry us away

and which would take us home again.
I *am* speaking for myself. Don't waste
your breath. The dogs aren't deaf,
they're trying to forget their names.

O-Dark-Hundred

All our mamas always said
don't it make your cross eyes stick
to pull that face. Plugged our fingers
in our ears and la-laed, now can't hear-hear
past our own blood's business, tinnitus,
ring-a-ding-whinging and waxing unbearable,
listless whistle, half mast status
quo don't quote me or cut – I know
that this requires more than my empathy.

I want to say a simple case of cause
and defective, cause and deflected,
defected, case in point and shoot,
in casualties and disaffected
and I do say, but imagine the words
not black and white but grey on grey.

One slippery sentence against another,
these little words sold by the truckload,
trafficked to tatters, twisted to shrapnel,
this little word wired to my waist
to blow this house all the way home.

Stare down the barrel of downward spiral,
past the smoking permutations,
smoldering mirrors, soul searches and seizures,
catch and erasure. I want to break
the vase made by the shape of the space
between two faces. What a joke.
As if it's between me and *between*.

Maybe I'll sleep by counting soldiers.
Yes, a game of names and numbers.
Give a guess. I'm thinking of a last
breath between – for sprawl's sake
let's narrow, take it from one of our own.
Now, no palaver, as the caveat is,
of course, *and counting*:

The Numbers Game

Alday Hartley Morrow Weeks
Farr Storey Long Ortiz
Little Turner Yearby Dearing
Holder Gooding Guerra Darling
Love Loveless Luckey Fester
Glimpse Gamble Time Balmer
Graves Galvan Galvez Day
Romeo Bravo Butcher Clay
Thrasher Crumpler Carver Settle
Rose Linden Ivy Nettles
Freeman Slaven Schiavoni
Payne Humble Holler Greenlee
Brown Blue Black White
Sun Moon Starr Light
Quill Hill Hull Hall
Ring Flint Waits Small
Winterbottom Springer
Summers McFall

[Note: This poem is composed of the surnames of U.S. troops killed in Iraq. These names represent, of course, only a tiny fraction of the dead.]

Let There Be a Firmament in the Midst of the Waters

Still the still, small voice, but also such
an unassuming sound of underbrush upon approach.

Often it's only after they enter the clearing
and unfurl that we look up to see what's coming.

The Fountains of the Deep and the Windows of Heaven

Once beneath a sure star, the mare with foal, as such,
I sat two horses. Underfoot, deadfall, and rings

for the firs' years of secret betrothal.
Once where darkness and its source

of moving water bred glowworms to wink out the contours'
coordinates, not "creeping thing" but wings' beginnings,

blue beacons to beckon a million no returns.
My clap turned their secrets back, took to black

like the city besieged. Such a stricken set, glutton
for the scrim and smolder. Shot stars slinking

with tucked tails to elsewhere's day. Once and still,
stone and water made such patient lovers, could call

first blush forever in the cave where above, below,
tried and try to touch their tongues together.

Forever? Forever.
All stigmas ripen to receive,

seasons of fruit each after its kind means here the bruised apple
of a bruised eye, here dear unshod mama and her sloshing
   seahorse.

This is the flower where I saw my first mountain on fire.
This is the stranger's electric perimeter.

Tricks to be taught by coins in a well,
once swallowed the wish's whisper whole.

Once under the roses, a rusty compass, .
sleepy secret still dreaming north.

Once under the roses, butterfly dust.
What once knew not to eat the wings?

The nighthawk strums the sunset
to a white-hot chord and in a real field I open

my bag of possibles, impossibles.
The real yellow grass casts real purple shadows.

Now all the parts reduce to finest ash, or rather,
once we were harder to scatter.

An Old Story

And still, no one has swept
the boot prints from the temple.

Began and Begins

Zeus, your x-rays won't verify.
Unearth the swaddled rock.
Quite painful passage, origins,
naturally. Misses lost kin.
Just in. His gut. Falters. Father's
eating dinner. Daddy's cloudy
belly-ballast. Aches. Again.

Awful big crybaby (*Da-da! Da-da!*)
each finger folds golden, holds
its jagged keep, little lightnings,
muted noise of piddling peals.
Quiet. Rest. (Red sundown, streamers
seeding storms, someday's sights set
to unset.) Virga won't wet, extinguish
(yet) your yellow zigzags, anything.

Floral Arrangements

No naming names but some people I know
spend all day decomposing. No

and for my next act and no *leave a message at the beep*
if you get my drift rather loam and sleep

and cut to the pit orchestra swelling into aftermath and
ever after. *She loves me or she loves me not* says Susan

with both black eyes sewn
shut. On one greeting card the yawning

kitten lolls on the settee and on another one a duck announces
   that he knows
some of the nicest people. I don't speak lightly when I say *how*

true. Hard rain on Johnny-Jump-Up and on Patient Lucy but their
   heads
bounce back. Dirge of bluebell and fiddlehead

claims of rest in peace early and rest in peace often
as even a nod-off

does you good. Lily to lily: *ever seen a gondola or a lot of elk*
all in one place? Lily to lily: *what's your favorite apostasy? Perhaps*
   I asked

you and forgot. Prune or the petunias grow rangy and don't just
   pull the withered petals
rather pinch the heads off at the stem. Just in case dress for a
   funeral.

Eat the hat and eat the heart out. Don't kill
the messengers who never claimed to be our bright ideas. Last will

and last won't last
are you going to eat that? Here comes the little engine chuff
    chuffing on its last

warm cockle. Some of the nicest people spend all day
    decomposing
hearts eaten out over the curtain down and always waiting

at stage right for the spotlight and the next big act. I never
    claimed to be
a baseball season. I'll go ahead and cry if that's my thing. When I
    said *can't miss me*

I'm the house with bougainvillea I meant
enormous purple flowers but even that

was wrong. *The* – and I quote – *small unnoticeable flowers
are produced in summer*

*and are surrounded
by large, brilliantly colored bracts.*

In Which These Truths
Hold Us to Be Self-Evident

Childhood's kudzu
Each summer's sudden
Can't see the true
Forest for the forest floor

Raised a too-small big top
Tent bulged up on
The backs of pachyderms

Trunks strangle-held
A labored being
Breathing in the heat

A huge herd
The woods rustled restless
Beneath a quiet
Designed to divine

So it seemed
To tumble off
The path would mean

A fall through
The vines' tightrope tangle
Tiger pit set canopy

Dressed as safety net
Into the real ravine
The deep-sea recesses
Below the deep-green seen

Ponte Sisto

Below the bridge,
an endless eddy
splashes back at the hem
of the spillway's skirt,
churns a froth
of sticks and milk jugs
and Styrofoam and soccer balls
and tarp and plastic bags
over and under
in a current bewitched
to vortex, backflow.
The river cannot
choose what
it cannot let go,
is low today
and seems unable
to part with anything
at all. On the bridge,
a woman wears
a gray blanket
and yells in no one's
particular direction.
The passersby part
to flow around her
body without touching
her body or the beggars or
their skinny dogs but stop
to turn and lean over
the guardrail and gawk
at the river's newfound
collection and speculate –
The contents of a wind-struck
campsite or trash of a more
northern town dragged

downstream, gathered here
through confluent accidents
of weather, water.
Or some impractical
joker's idea
of art –
the bouncing balls
of a lunatic lottery,
re-arrangement, de-
composition, ever un-
still life, inconsolable
and constant star-crossed
constellation, construct
of awkward orbits, collisions.
The passersby watch
for their favorite pieces
of flotsam to pop up
again and then do
what passersby do
(pass by).
The hungry dogs watch
their hungry masters
who watch the possibly
unwatched pockets
and the woman stops yelling
at no one to look up
at no one, reach
beneath her blanket
and touch herself.

Missive

My everything I say but don't be silly.
How could everything possibly be mine?

The future's on her belly in the dust
laying for the stagecoach sweet-talking the scope.

The past? Don't let me catch that sniveling
misnomer here. From now on I'm calling her

the gone as in *in the gone I could not know
to hold you*. If you were my and I your charge

a life before as well I hope at least
I had a fabulous hat and a language

with which to say *believe me*. Maybe no stranger
than stepping from one room into another.

Maybe *I thirst*. I'll drink to in and out
of breath to excess to your last ash.

Tale too tall for me to tiptoe reach
the top shelf bottle there with our name on it.

I don't need to spill it spell it out.
You know our name by now don't you? My love

as a prescribed burn a *this hurts me more than*
a cause the cone to open. Welter swelter

split the deck of cards. Can't predict king
or jack but that you'll pull the black and I

the redder riddles. If you are reading this
you can't be nearly close enough to me.

A Way

Without you I am making up an ocean.

Any resemblance to real oceans living or dead
is purely coincidental.
                              I'm calling it *swimmingly*
but I lie.
              Distance and its usual glitter.

Names have been changed to protect the innocent.

My ocean is always on my other left.

Closer my own toes clumsy ghosts startle
the fry in my tide pools to skitter little
to nothing and so still again.
                              All oceans
are subject to change without notice.
                              All
oceans are proofs solved in whispers.
                              No one
can marry an ocean although anyone can propose.

Kelp and paua bits and paua pieces
and green glass worn to a stone of its old self.

My ocean is neither express nor implied.

I meant to make some *us* up earlier.

All oceans are studies in revision.

My ocean is trying to say nothing.

Core Despondence

Dear luminous occlusion,
my numen – a question.

What to do with all this ocean?
Mussels in a dream mean

minor gains, nothing to
keep my eyes on low

tide for. Bleached snail shells
to dust on the high hills spell

out *waves was here*. The sun?
I'm looking into it. The sum

of tongue plus tongue
become an IOU

on parchment paper.
Was you and I swapped sugar

for swelter, time before
this present tense. Dear

speaking of talking
about this life feels to take

a lifetime, which word is is normal
here. This pen pals pales

to once in our matryoshka.
Some silly buoy, single sundry

and dare say life-like island.
Dear I'd say spit-side up send

your stamp business end to my
far shore but they say

no one licks anything anymore.

The Eel

After Montale

A siren sprung to heed
some unsung self-same song
beats back the Baltic again
again to take her leave
by force of frozen seas
and move to meet
our rivers' warmer mouths.
Her body in and up
against the gradient
the current insistent
artery to capillary always
more within and ever
flexed to any vessel even
as the last lumen
breaks granite's
near-impenetrable heart.
Even now through beds
of mud and muck until
at last sun struck off
a chestnut's tinder
kindles a flicker
in barely a ditch slipped
from the slope
of the Apennine spine
and on to the Romagna.
It is our eel our lit whip
our arrow feathered with fire
and let fly like an *amen*.
Unlikely midwife
from the gullies' slime
and parched creeks
of the Pyrenees it's she
alone would birth
a green breath back

The Eel

seek life in a charred fist
still and in the sucked sludge
of the lungs gone under.
She is the wick whose spark
says *start again*
again says all begins
when all looks wrack and ash:
her glimpsed glint twin
to the flash your lashes frame
to shine intact from the sinkhole
slop-trough no-man's-land
where every son
of every man remains
interred –

        you can't come clean
        and kiss your sister?

City Beach

Your mouth said so long from so long said high
tide's not a timid girl is what is missing.
I could clap flippers skip the asterisk
and hop a plane. Some mouths say nets and not
nets to trust around anyone's daughter.
Ask what's on tap in the shape of a ship.
A mouth in a bottle is no kiss sealed
to sender. In it remainders and no answer
and a thin relic at that. Any ocean
is old enough to know better. Your mouth
to mine is departures arrivals a flawless ledger.
Some mouths say swim at your own risk say salt
again is stingy dinner. My mouth remains
a faithful measure. Some mouths say shark
in shallow water but I suspect the waves
wash in on empty and someone had to
truck in all this sand from elsewhere here.

Note: Heavy Penalties Exist for False Declarations

Do NOT feed the lizards.
Do NOT flush the hand towels.

Lungs are needy pets to lug through air
but who would love them here

like I do? The seeds and snails and soil are for my mother.
A snow globe is a lovely souvenir, but so too tortoise shells, tubers,

bamboo, rattan, rhizomes, noodles, rice.
Less headlong, lest long face,

they say, but I'm not from around here. They don't mean
what I mean by "uplifted." They drink it with cinnamon.

They do an adorable war dance. Not flight,
but flight-like. I'd like you to meet

my natural predators. If you guessed
"delicate cycle," you'd be wrong. Tiptoes are their best toes, but
    I'm a mess

of tenterhooks, raw in the middle with a terrible salad, eggshells,
    brass tacks.
I admit, I have been to the dairy, the abattoir, the forest and back,

my duffel packed with pine cones and potpourri,
budwood and bulbs, wax, wool, tusks, ghee,

and fifty-one cigars. I want whatever's on my cleats.
I'd rather leave these thumbs behind. It's your dime, I'm just
    turning on it,

I said, but they weren't familiar with dimes.
Let's play something to pass the time:

one word comes from "to strike down,"
the other, "to go over," meaning "memory."

Dreaming in New Zealand

I love this tongue as mine (is mine)
and would all were as I am wont
to hear here: sex, a quest, great grail,
for I hear *seeks*, with no sweat spent
to search that isn't *sweet*, as every
beck and call's both song and beak
with which to hold our tune. Winter
wears her well-earned warrior's clothes,
a season wearing thinner, wetter,
colder, but still and ever green, here –
she'd not leave her leaves, not shed
what's hers though the southerly
tried and tries to whistle them away.
And since this is my comedy
of ears, in one and in the other's
fate's to trip again, I'll claim:
the body is both bread and breed,
as words well said are planted seed
and grow so where we tread is treed,
where each line read remains the reed
on which the note is played when pressed
to lips, mouth, self-ordained as priest,
weds *wed* to *we'd* and *weed* and so
with word grown one forever as even
the dead remain in deed, wound round
and round in these wet sheets of wind.

Long Distance

Today, I take a nap in my afternoon.
It is, of course, the middle of your night.
I lie on my back and imagine us lying back-to-back.
As hemispheres have it, we are.
My shoulder blades are almost up against yours.
The soles of our feet are almost pressed together.
Only the world is in between us.
In your morning, you sweep up glass
where a dove mistook a pane for nothing at all.
In my evening, I hear the call of a stitchbird,
endemic, endangered (extinct on the mainland),
previously thought to be a member of the honeyeater family,
recently revealed to have no close living relative at all.
It is the only bird known to mate face-to-face.
Its Maori name is "hihi," meaning "ray."
("Hihi o te ra": "sunbeam." "Hihi kokiri": "x-ray.")
"Hihi," pronounced one giggle, not two greetings.

Fair Play

Black rocks, red rocks.

White lichen and rot.

The trees wear
sleeves of moss.

The moss wears
a sheath of droplets
and a coat of fog.

The fog swans about
the valley until noon.

Then, wind, all
swither and swerve.

Some trick to sing
the breath away,
then swing back
in and sling it
through magnified
times more and more
so, oh troubled
ooh to the nth.

Sheet web
and spider
waits under.

Fair Play

Orb web
and spider waits
offstage with a leg
on a thread spun
from the center.

Grey warbler
hovers mid-air,
builds to a trill
that falls and rises,
plucks the spider
and the web as well,
harvests the thread
to bind less a nest
than a structure.

Rootlets, leaves, grass
coaxed and hung
bulb-shaped,
feather-lined.

Inside, two eggs.

The smaller is its own.

The larger, the cuckoo's
switcheroo, soon-to-be
insatiable foundling.

Mistletoe, too,
knows from opportune,
plants its seeds
to the bark
with a sticky kiss,

then settles in to suck
its host's sweet
everything.

Cat takes to
the woods, can't see
her penance, but
smells it close.

Her owner has tied
the dead finch
tight to her collar,
broken neck to neck.

The faster she runs,
the more it flaps
against her throat.

Fiddleheads unfurl
fractal, furred fronds
curl their hearts out,
a million question
marks set to the sun
and soon to exclaim
all the way open.

Fleet of spiderlings
unspools to catch
and be caught by
the current, wind,
which lifts the strings
and scatters, drops
the bodies a-field
like leaflets too tiny

for proper propaganda,
more like prayers
inscribed on
grains of rice –

let us at least attempt
our impossibly
tiny lives.

Index of Titles and First Lines

A Note About the Author

Dora Malech was born in New Haven, Connecticut in 1981 and grew up in Bethesda, Maryland. She earned a BA in Fine Arts from Yale College in 2003 and an MFA in Poetry from the University of Iowa Writers' Workshop in 2005. She has been the recipient of a Frederick M. Clapp Poetry Writing Fellowship from Yale, a Truman Capote Fellowship and a Teaching-Writing Fellowship from the Writers' Workshop, a Glenn Schaeffer Award in Poetry, and a Writer's Fellowship at the Civitella Ranieri Center in Umbertide, Italy. Her poems have appeared in numerous publications, including the *New Yorker*, *Poetry*, *Best New Poets*, *American Letters & Commentary*, *Poetry London*, and the *Yale Review*. She has taught writing at the University of Iowa; Victoria University's International Institute of Modern Letters in Wellington, New Zealand; Kirkwood Community College in Cedar Rapids, Iowa; and Augustana College in Rock Island, Illinois. She lives in Iowa City.